1996

A History of

AIRCRAFT

Other Books in the Series:

A History of Powered Ships
A History of Sailing Ships
A History of Water Travel

A HISTORY OF AIRCRAFT

Text by Cristiana Leoni

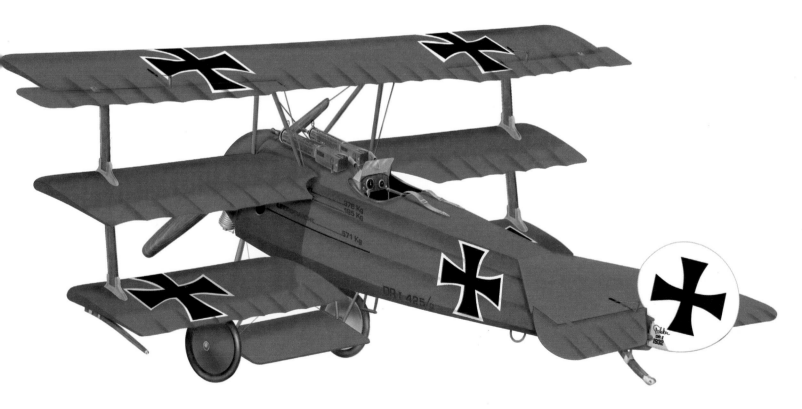

BLACKBIRCH PRESS

An imprint of Thomson Gale, a part of The Thomson Corporation

MAR 3 1 2008

Detroit • New York • San Francisco • San Diego • New Haven, Conn. • Waterville, Maine • London • Munich

Conception and production: Andrea Dué s.r.l.
Text: Cristiana Leoni
Translation: Erika Pauli
Illustrations: Alessandro Baldanzi, Alessandro Bartolozzi, Leonello Calvetti, Lorenzo Cecchi, Gian Paolo Faleschini, Azzurra Giacomelli, Sauro Giampaia, Luigi Ieracitano, Roberto Simoni, Research, documentation, and layout: Luigi Ieracitano
Cutouts: Uliana Derniatina

Photo Credits: Page 10: Hulton-Deutsch Collection/Corbis/Contrasto; pages 41, 43: courtesy of NASA

For more information, contact
Blackbirch Press
27500 Drake Rd.
Farmington Hills, MI 48331-3535
Or you can visit our Internet site at http://www.gale.com

LIBRARY OF CONGRESS CATALOGING-IN-PUBLICATION DATA

Leoni, Cristiana.
  A history of aircraft / by Cristiana Leoni.
    p. cm. — (Moving people, things, and ideas)
  Includes bibliographical references and index.
  ISBN 1-4103-0659-3 (hardcover : alk. paper)
  1. Airplanes—History—Juvenile literature. I. Title. II. Series.

  TL670.3.L47 2005
  629.133'09—dc22

                                                  2005001845

Contents

Flying

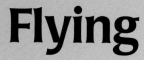

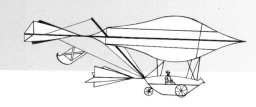

The first motorized airplane flight took place just a little more than 100 years ago. In the century since that first flight, flying has become the fastest and safest method of transportation. Engineers have created aircraft that travel faster than the speed of sound. They have built rockets that propel people beyond Earth's atmosphere to explore space. Airplanes changed the world. They made the planet seem like a smaller place because they allowed people and goods to move quickly from one place to another. They changed the way wars were fought. After airplanes were invented, controlling the skies became one of the most important goals during war. The work that led to human flight began a long time ago when people began trying to invent contraptions that would fly.

An Englishman named Sir George Cayley made studies that were important in the development of flight. At left is a picture of his propeller-powered airship. Above is a drawing of a glider he built in 1853.

Above: This glider was built from drawings made in the late 1400s by Leonardo da Vinci. Da Vinci was a painter, engineer, mathematician, and architect. He looked at the wings of birds and bats to design his flying machines.

Below, left: In 1874, the French navy officer Felix Du Temple built a flying machine with fixed wings that was powered by a steam engine. The contraption lurched into the air, then fell back to Earth.

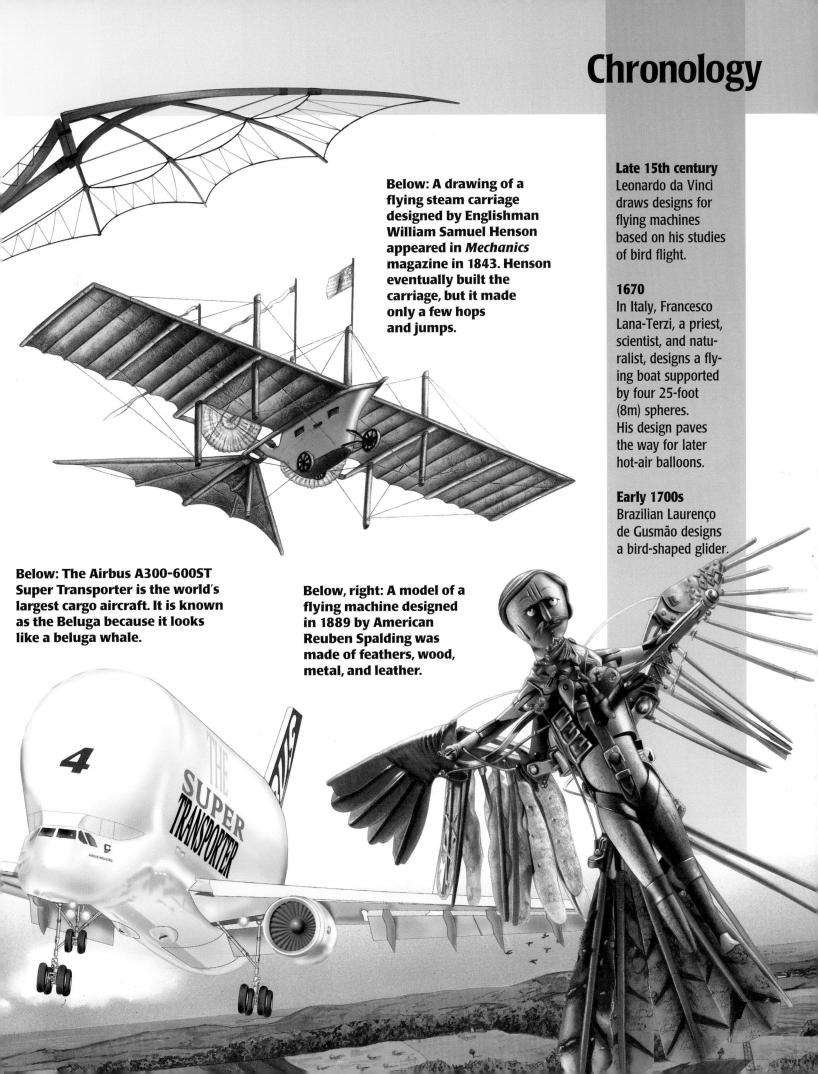

Chronology

Below: A drawing of a flying steam carriage designed by Englishman William Samuel Henson appeared in *Mechanics* magazine in 1843. Henson eventually built the carriage, but it made only a few hops and jumps.

Below: The Airbus A300-600ST Super Transporter is the world's largest cargo aircraft. It is known as the Beluga because it looks like a beluga whale.

Below, right: A model of a flying machine designed in 1889 by American Reuben Spalding was made of feathers, wood, metal, and leather.

Late 15th century
Leonardo da Vinci draws designs for flying machines based on his studies of bird flight.

1670
In Italy, Francesco Lana-Terzi, a priest, scientist, and naturalist, designs a flying boat supported by four 25-foot (8m) spheres. His design paves the way for later hot-air balloons.

Early 1700s
Brazilian Laurenço de Gusmão designs a bird-shaped glider.

Lighter than Air

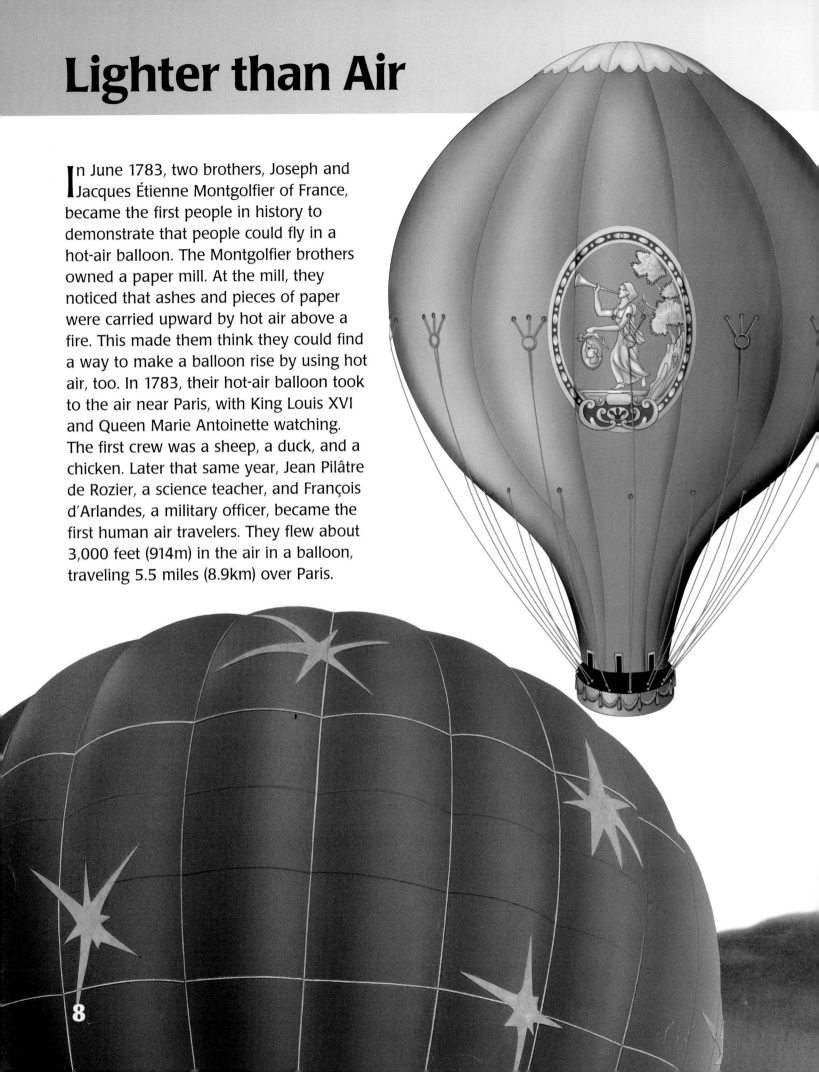

In June 1783, two brothers, Joseph and Jacques Étienne Montgolfier of France, became the first people in history to demonstrate that people could fly in a hot-air balloon. The Montgolfier brothers owned a paper mill. At the mill, they noticed that ashes and pieces of paper were carried upward by hot air above a fire. This made them think they could find a way to make a balloon rise by using hot air, too. In 1783, their hot-air balloon took to the air near Paris, with King Louis XVI and Queen Marie Antoinette watching. The first crew was a sheep, a duck, and a chicken. Later that same year, Jean Pilâtre de Rozier, a science teacher, and François d'Arlandes, a military officer, became the first human air travelers. They flew about 3,000 feet (914m) in the air in a balloon, traveling 5.5 miles (8.9km) over Paris.

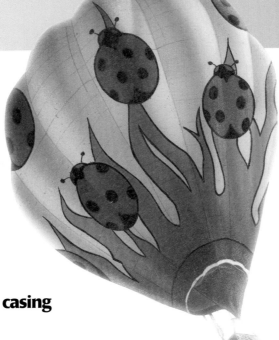

Left: The Montgolfier brothers' blue balloon with gold decoration was made of linen fabric and paper. Other balloons on this page were used for demonstrations and celebrations.

Below: The main parts of a balloon are shown here.

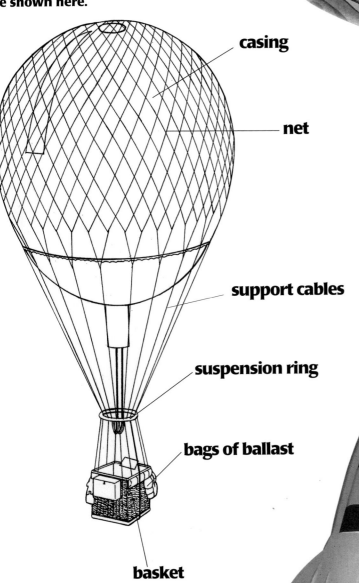

casing

net

support cables

suspension ring

bags of ballast

basket

1766
Englishman Henry Cavendish discovers hydrogen.

November 1783
Jean Pilâtre de Rozier and François d'Arlandes fly for 25 minutes above Paris in a hot-air balloon equipped with a burner.

December 1783
Jacques Charles's hydrogen balloon flies over Paris for nearly an hour.

January 1785
A hydrogen balloon flies over the English Channel for the first time.

Airships

In 1852, the French engineer Henry Giffard flew the first airship. Airships are huge crafts that are able to fly because they are filled with a gas that is lighter than air. Giffard's airship was filled with hydrogen gas and powered by a steam engine.

In 1900, Count Ferdinand Graf von Zeppelin first flew another type of airship in Germany. His airships were called zeppelins, and they became the most famous airships in the world. The huge zeppelins were filled with hydrogen gas. Engines like those in cars turned propellers to power the zeppelins. The zeppelins were huge, about 420 feet (128m) long—longer than a football field. During World War I, Germans used zeppelins as bombers. In 1910, a zeppelin became the first commercial airship—customers paid to travel on it. In the 1930s, zeppelins were thought to be the height of luxury in flying. Zeppelins had dining rooms, libraries, and lounges with grand pianos.

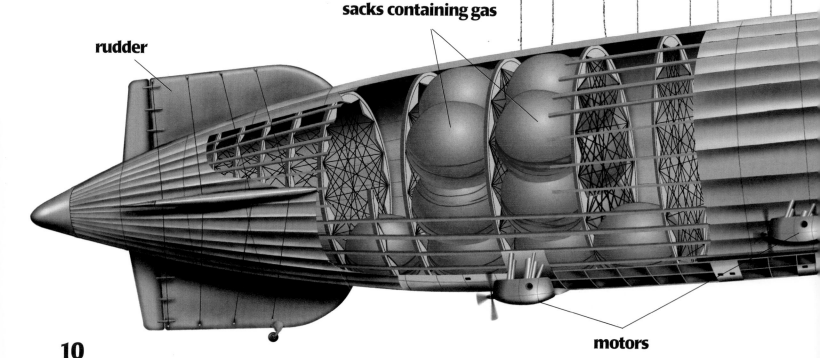

Above: A drawing shows a reconstruction of Henry Giffard's airship.

sacks containing gas

rudder

motors

Chronology

1898
The Zeppelin
airship-building
firm is founded
in Germany.

1909
DELAG, the first
airline company in
the world, is found-
ed in Germany.
It operates a fleet
of airships.

August 1929
The airship *Graf
Zeppelin* begins
transatlantic service
to North and South
America.

May 6, 1937
The *Hindenburg*
catches fire as it
attempts to land
in New Jersey.

1940
The era of airship
travel ends, and
zeppelins are
destroyed.

**Below: This pic-
ture shows the
interior of an
airship. Airtight
compartments
filled with gas
take up most of
the space.**

gondola

passenger deck

In May 1936, the zeppelin *Hindenburg* took its maiden flight, a 60-hour trip from Germany to New Jersey. But on May 6, 1937, after ten successful round trips, the *Hindenburg* exploded into flames as it attempted to land in Lakehurst, New Jersey. The disaster killed 35 of the 97 people on board and one member of the ground crew. It signaled the end of the commercial use of zeppelins.

The airships still flying today are called blimps. Companies use them for advertising or to provide aerial pictures of sporting events. Modern blimps are different from the old zeppelins. They do not have a stiff frame, as the zeppelins did. Airships now use helium, a gas that is lighter than air but does not catch fire as easily as hydrogen.

On May 6, 1937, the *Hindenburg* burst into flames as it attempted to land at Lakehurst, New Jersey. The cause of the fire was never found.

Above: The *Hindenburg* was the pride of Germany.

Right: The spire of the Empire State Building in New York City was originally designed as a mooring post for airships. It was never used for this purpose, though.

13

The First Flight

The first human flight in a heavier-than-air machine took place on the windswept, sandy dunes of Kitty Hawk, North Carolina, on December 17, 1903. The flight lasted barely twelve seconds and covered just 120 feet (37m), but it was an event that changed the world. Wilbur and Orville Wright, brothers who ran a bicycle shop in Ohio, created the airplane that reached this milestone. The brothers had been fascinated by the idea of flying since their childhood, when their father had given them a small helicopter-like toy that was powered by a rubber band. They built kites and gliders and many experimental contraptions before coming up with their *Flyer*. At Kitty Hawk, they proved that their invention could fly on its own power and could be controlled by a pilot. It was made from wood and canvas. Its propellers were connected by a bicycle chain. It was powered by a small engine. Though the two mechanics had little formal scientific training, they succeeded in finding a way for people to fly.

Below: The Wright brothers carried out their flight experiments with the help of friends and other supporters.

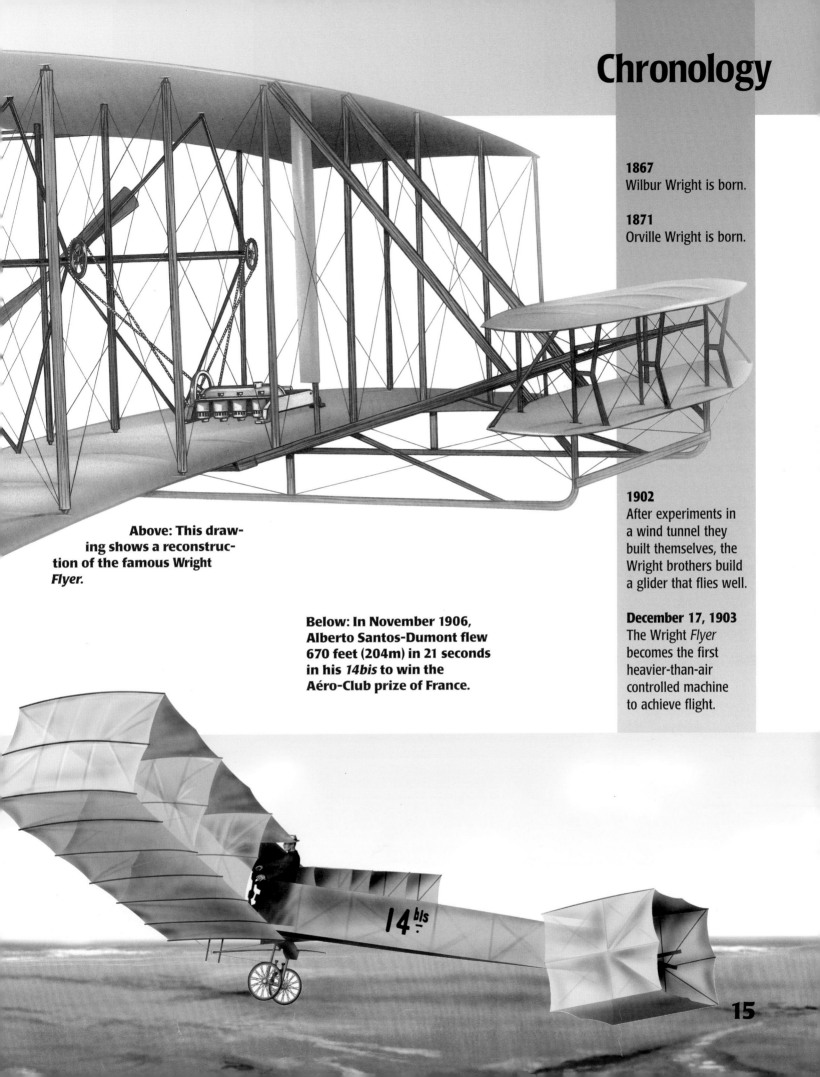

Chronology

1867
Wilbur Wright is born.

1871
Orville Wright is born.

1902
After experiments in a wind tunnel they built themselves, the Wright brothers build a glider that flies well.

December 17, 1903
The Wright *Flyer* becomes the first heavier-than-air controlled machine to achieve flight.

Above: This drawing shows a reconstruction of the famous Wright *Flyer*.

Below: In November 1906, Alberto Santos-Dumont flew 670 feet (204m) in 21 seconds in his *14bis* to win the Aéro-Club prize of France.

World War I

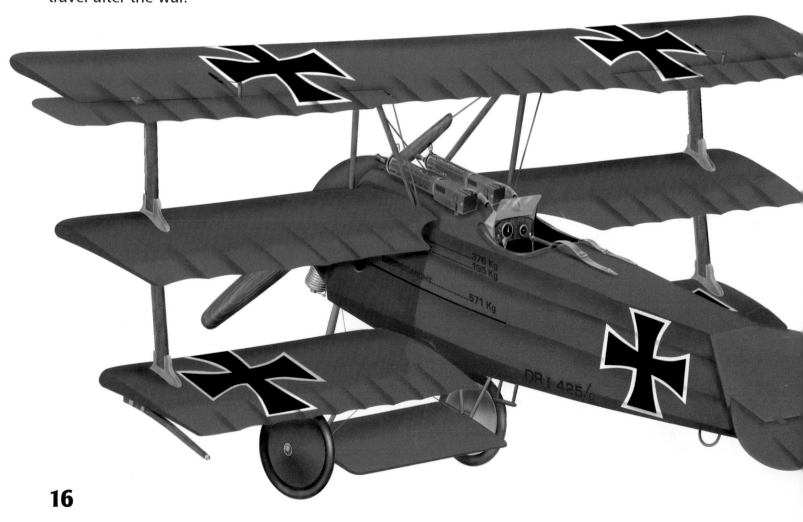

When World War I broke out in 1914, flying was still an experimental activity. Planes were made of canvas and wood. They had top speeds of less than 150 miles (240km) per hour. But airplanes quickly changed the way war was fought. Planes introduced the world to a new battleground: the air. Earlier wars had been fought on land and sea. World War I led to technological advancements in airplanes, too. The changes in the way airplanes were designed and built led to commercial air travel after the war.

Above: A picture shows the twin-engine, all-metal Voisin LA III. This French aircraft was the first to be used to shoot down an enemy airplane in World War I.

Below: The Fokker Dr I (or Fokker Eindecker) was the most well-known German fighter plane of World War I. Manfred von Richthofen was the most famous pilot of this plane. He was nicknamed the Red Baron because he shot down so many enemy planes.

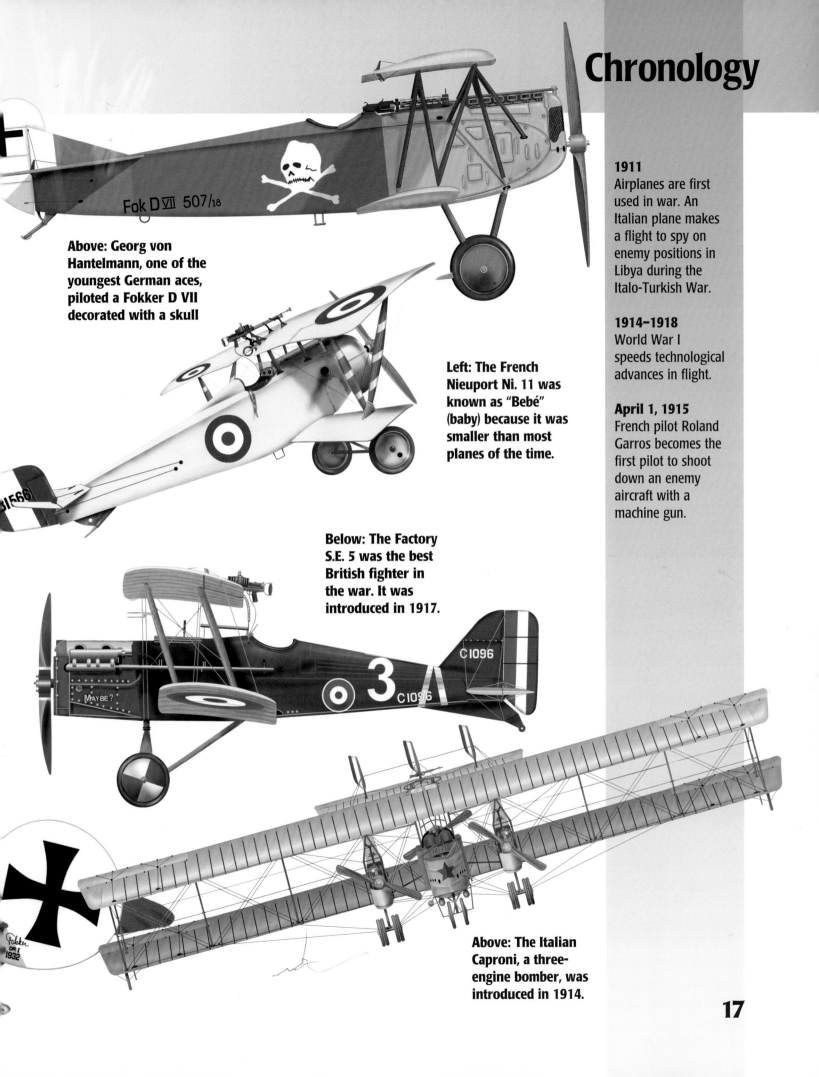

Fok D VII 507/18

Above: Georg von Hantelmann, one of the youngest German aces, piloted a Fokker D VII decorated with a skull

Left: The French Nieuport Ni. 11 was known as "Bebé" (baby) because it was smaller than most planes of the time.

Below: The Factory S.E. 5 was the best British fighter in the war. It was introduced in 1917.

C1096

3 C1096

MAYBE?

1911
Airplanes are first used in war. An Italian plane makes a flight to spy on enemy positions in Libya during the Italo-Turkish War.

1914–1918
World War I speeds technological advances in flight.

April 1, 1915
French pilot Roland Garros becomes the first pilot to shoot down an enemy aircraft with a machine gun.

Above: The Italian Caproni, a three-engine bomber, was introduced in 1914.

The First Airlines

After World War I, people began to think about how airplanes could be used in business. They knew planes could be used to deliver goods to far-away destinations quickly. People could buy tickets to travel on planes. In 1911, the British became the first to test an airline business when they tried delivering mail by plane in India. By 1919, airline companies were being formed across the world.

The first airline companies often used converted World War I bombers. Traveling by planes in the early days of commercial flight was very different from traveling by plane today. The converted bombers were cold, because they were not insulated from the cold air outside the plane. The flights were bumpy because the planes could not fly into the calmer air in higher altitudes where planes fly today. Early runways were often nothing more than strips of grass. And some airports were sheds.

Above: Ford, a company best known for its automobiles, also manufactured an airplane. The Tin Goose, as it was known, was one of the first all-metal aircraft.

Above, right: The Junkers F13 was the first all-metal airplane built specifically for carrying passengers. The aircraft could carry four passengers in its heated cabin.

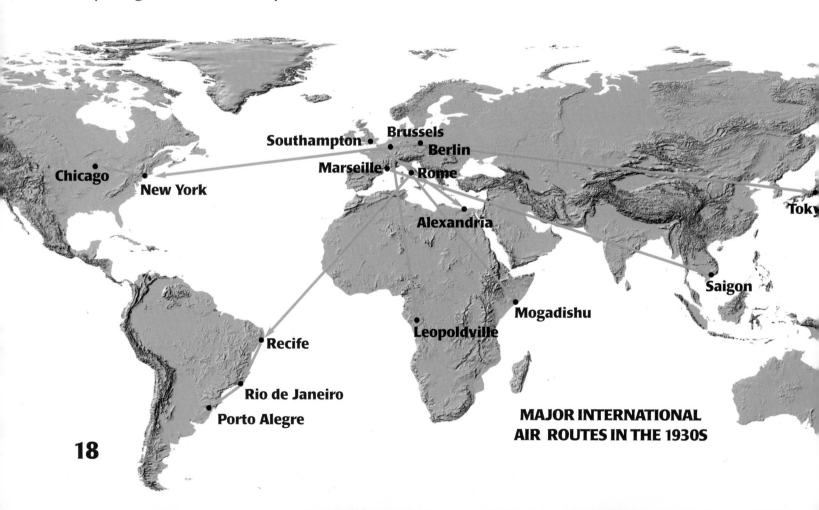

Southampton • Brussels • Berlin
Marseille • Rome
Chicago • New York
Alexandria
Toky[o]
Saigon
Mogadishu
Leopoldville
Recife
Rio de Janeiro
Porto Alegre

MAJOR INTERNATIONAL AIR ROUTES IN THE 1930S

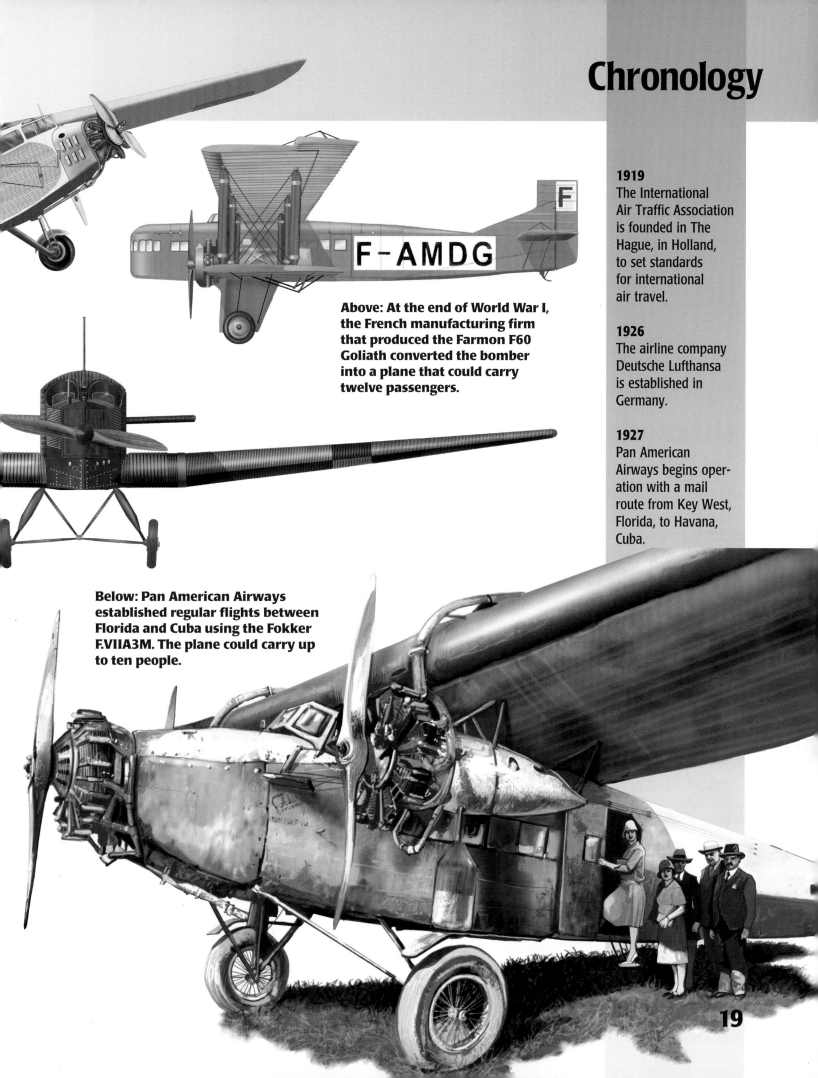

F-AMDG

Above: At the end of World War I, the French manufacturing firm that produced the Farmon F60 Goliath converted the bomber into a plane that could carry twelve passengers.

1919
The International Air Traffic Association is founded in The Hague, in Holland, to set standards for international air travel.

1926
The airline company Deutsche Lufthansa is established in Germany.

1927
Pan American Airways begins operation with a mail route from Key West, Florida, to Havana, Cuba.

Below: Pan American Airways established regular flights between Florida and Cuba using the Fokker F.VIIA3M. The plane could carry up to ten people.

Pioneers

On May 21, 1927, a 25-year-old pilot named Charles Lindbergh became the first person to fly a solo nonstop flight from New York to Paris. The historic 3,600-mile (5,794km) flight lasted 33 hours and 30 minutes. The feat won him a $25,000 prize and fame as one of aviation's most important pioneers. Lindbergh flew in a single-engine plane named the *Spirit of St. Louis*, after the city where his financial backers were based. Because the fuel tanks were located in front of the cockpit, Lindbergh could not see what was in front of him as he flew, except by using a periscope. He carried only the equipment he considered necessary: four sandwiches, two canteens of water, and 451 gallons (1,707L) of gas. He decided not to carry a parachute or radio so he could carry more gas. Along the way he became very tired. He flew through fog. Sleet began to cling to his plane. When he landed, he was greeted by crowds of people cheering his heroic feat.

Above: Built in Germany in 1929, the Dornier Do X was the largest seaplane of its day. The seaplane, with its three floors, sleeping cabins, bathrooms, and dining rooms, carried 169 passengers on its first flight. The plane had many mechanical problems, and it was very expensive to fly because it used so much fuel.

Right: On July 15, 1933, Italo Balbo, an Italian general, led a squadron of 24 Savoia-Marchetti S. 55X seaplanes from Italy to Illinois. The odd-looking planes, with their double hulls and engines facing both forward and backward, landed on Lake Michigan in Chicago to the cheers of crowds.

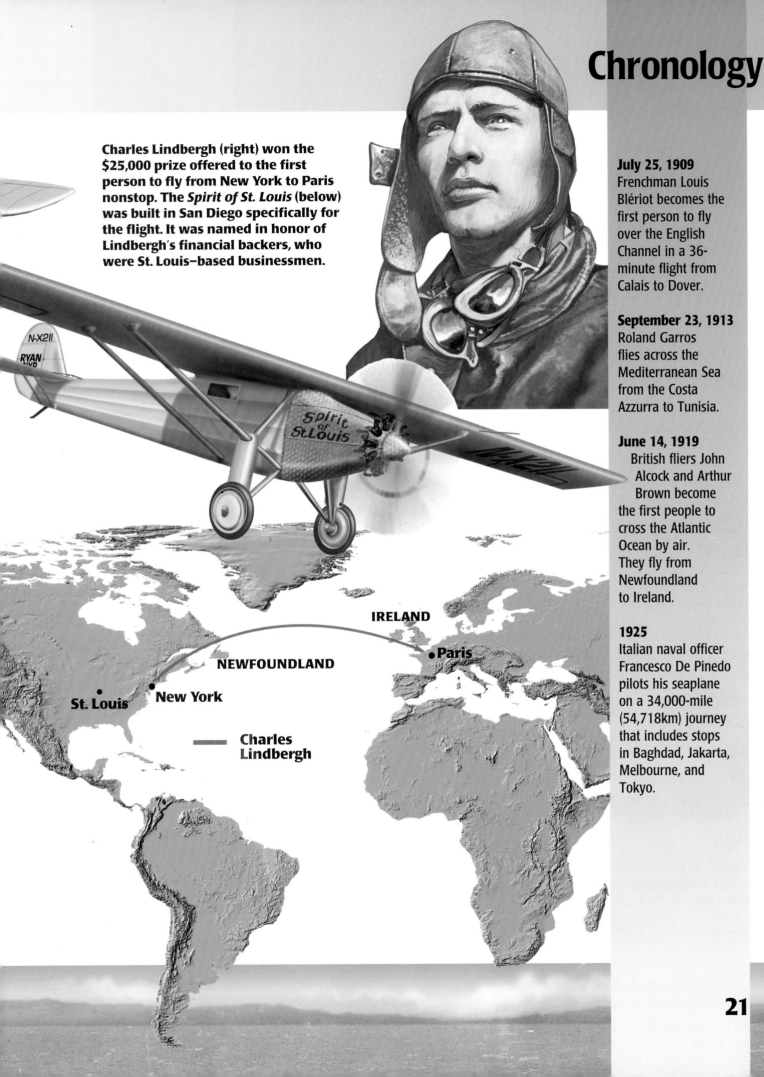

Chronology

Charles Lindbergh (right) won the $25,000 prize offered to the first person to fly from New York to Paris nonstop. The *Spirit of St. Louis* (below) was built in San Diego specifically for the flight. It was named in honor of Lindbergh's financial backers, who were St. Louis–based businessmen.

July 25, 1909
Frenchman Louis Blériot becomes the first person to fly over the English Channel in a 36-minute flight from Calais to Dover.

September 23, 1913
Roland Garros flies across the Mediterranean Sea from the Costa Azzurra to Tunisia.

June 14, 1919
British fliers John Alcock and Arthur Brown become the first people to cross the Atlantic Ocean by air. They fly from Newfoundland to Ireland.

1925
Italian naval officer Francesco De Pinedo pilots his seaplane on a 34,000-mile (54,718km) journey that includes stops in Baghdad, Jakarta, Melbourne, and Tokyo.

IRELAND

Paris

NEWFOUNDLAND

St. Louis New York

—— Charles Lindbergh

World War II

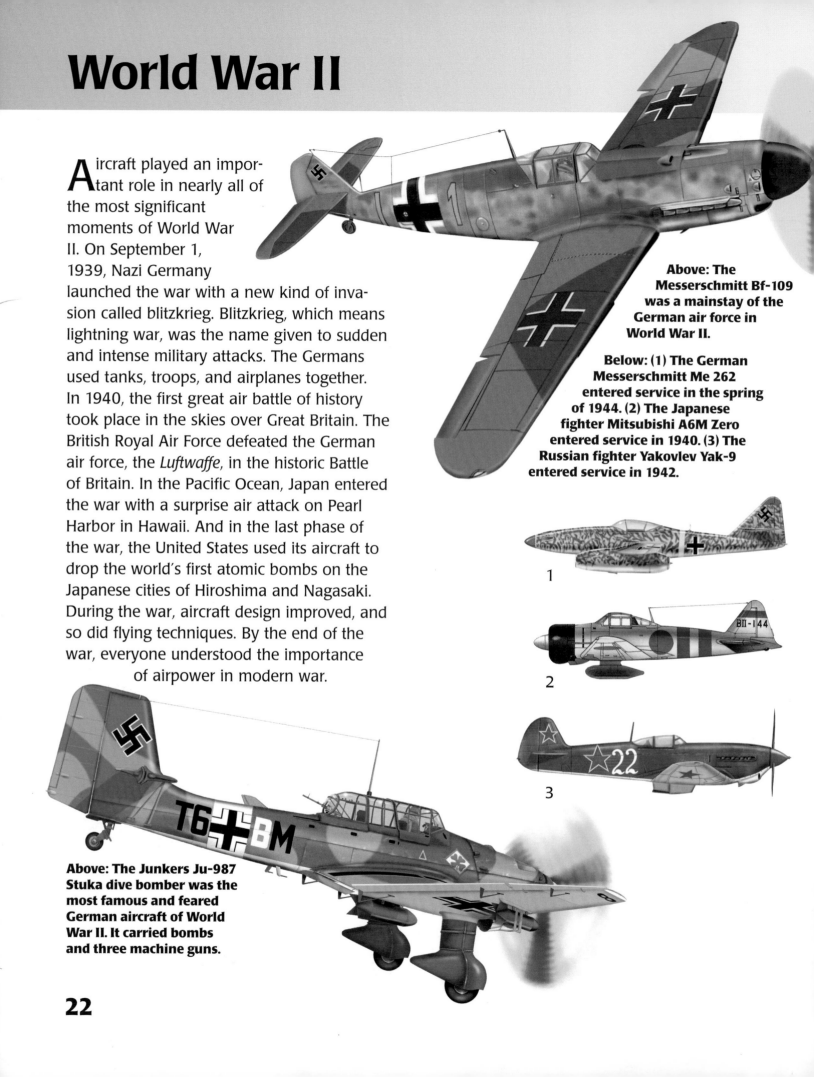

Aircraft played an important role in nearly all of the most significant moments of World War II. On September 1, 1939, Nazi Germany launched the war with a new kind of invasion called blitzkrieg. Blitzkrieg, which means lightning war, was the name given to sudden and intense military attacks. The Germans used tanks, troops, and airplanes together. In 1940, the first great air battle of history took place in the skies over Great Britain. The British Royal Air Force defeated the German air force, the *Luftwaffe*, in the historic Battle of Britain. In the Pacific Ocean, Japan entered the war with a surprise air attack on Pearl Harbor in Hawaii. And in the last phase of the war, the United States used its aircraft to drop the world's first atomic bombs on the Japanese cities of Hiroshima and Nagasaki. During the war, aircraft design improved, and so did flying techniques. By the end of the war, everyone understood the importance of airpower in modern war.

Above: The Messerschmitt Bf-109 was a mainstay of the German air force in World War II.

Below: (1) The German Messerschmitt Me 262 entered service in the spring of 1944. (2) The Japanese fighter Mitsubishi A6M Zero entered service in 1940. (3) The Russian fighter Yakovlev Yak-9 entered service in 1942.

1

2

3

Above: The Junkers Ju-987 Stuka dive bomber was the most famous and feared German aircraft of World War II. It carried bombs and three machine guns.

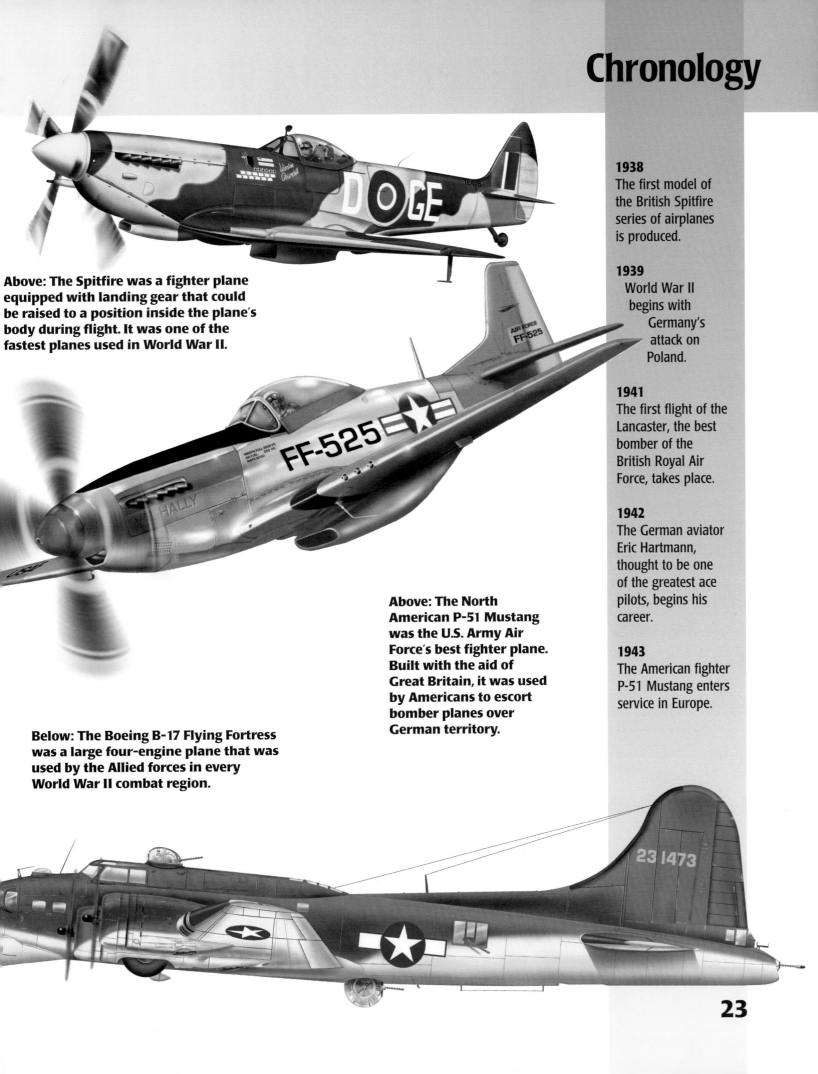

Above: The Spitfire was a fighter plane equipped with landing gear that could be raised to a position inside the plane's body during flight. It was one of the fastest planes used in World War II.

Above: The North American P-51 Mustang was the U.S. Army Air Force's best fighter plane. Built with the aid of Great Britain, it was used by Americans to escort bomber planes over German territory.

Below: The Boeing B-17 Flying Fortress was a large four-engine plane that was used by the Allied forces in every World War II combat region.

1938
The first model of the British Spitfire series of airplanes is produced.

1939
World War II begins with Germany's attack on Poland.

1941
The first flight of the Lancaster, the best bomber of the British Royal Air Force, takes place.

1942
The German aviator Eric Hartmann, thought to be one of the greatest ace pilots, begins his career.

1943
The American fighter P-51 Mustang enters service in Europe.

Air Travel After World War II

World War II sped technological improvements in aircraft designs. One of these was cabins that pumped in pressurized air. Usually at high altitudes, the air is too thin to supply people with all the oxygen their bodies need. Pressurized air, though, allows people to breathe in enough oxygen at high altitudes. New airplanes that used pressurized air could fly faster, farther, and at higher altitudes than older planes.

Right: The Lockheed Constellation, nicknamed Connie, was one of the most modern four-engine planes of its day. A military version of the plane was introduced in 1943. The Super G version carried enough fuel to allow it to make the first commercial nonstop flights between New York City and Los Angeles.

Left: In 1930, United Airlines first began using hostesses on board its planes. The first hostesses or stewardesses were required to be nurses.

Below: A drawing shows passengers boarding an aircraft in the years after World War II.

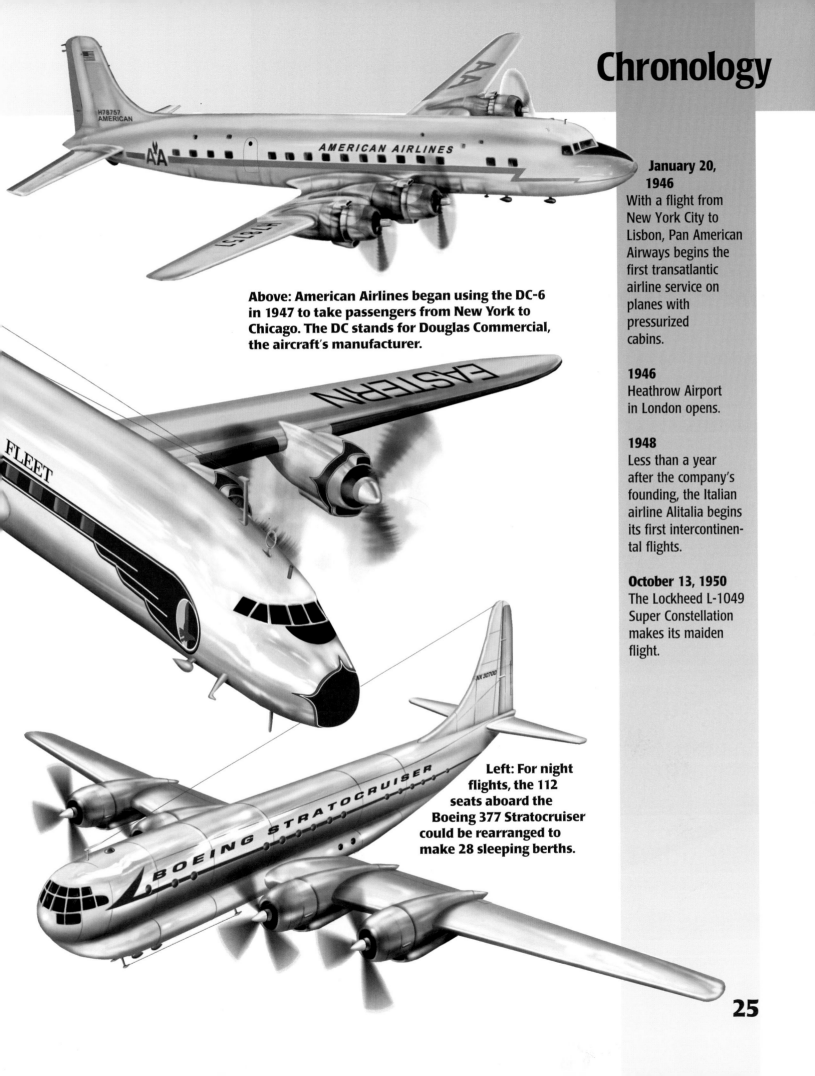

Above: American Airlines began using the DC-6 in 1947 to take passengers from New York to Chicago. The DC stands for Douglas Commercial, the aircraft's manufacturer.

January 20, 1946
With a flight from New York City to Lisbon, Pan American Airways begins the first transatlantic airline service on planes with pressurized cabins.

1946
Heathrow Airport in London opens.

1948
Less than a year after the company's founding, the Italian airline Alitalia begins its first intercontinental flights.

October 13, 1950
The Lockheed L-1049 Super Constellation makes its maiden flight.

Left: For night flights, the 112 seats aboard the Boeing 377 Stratocruiser could be rearranged to make 28 sleeping berths.

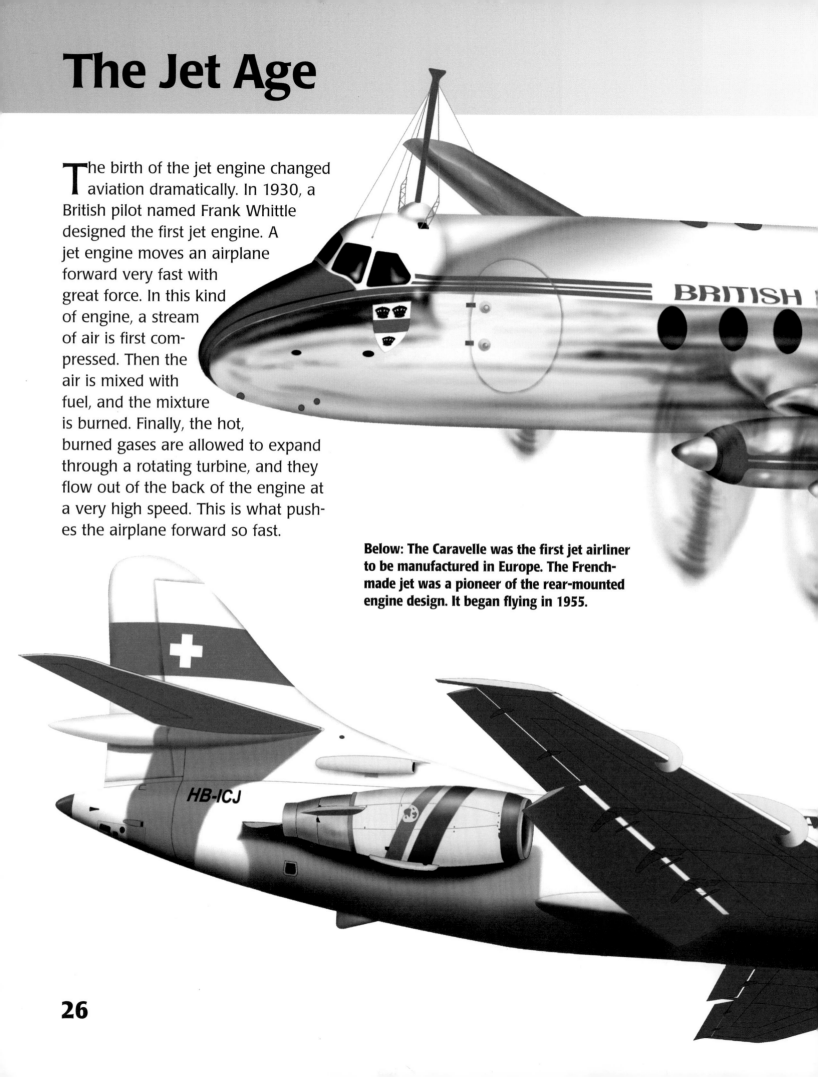

The Jet Age

The birth of the jet engine changed aviation dramatically. In 1930, a British pilot named Frank Whittle designed the first jet engine. A jet engine moves an airplane forward very fast with great force. In this kind of engine, a stream of air is first compressed. Then the air is mixed with fuel, and the mixture is burned. Finally, the hot, burned gases are allowed to expand through a rotating turbine, and they flow out of the back of the engine at a very high speed. This is what pushes the airplane forward so fast.

Below: The Caravelle was the first jet airliner to be manufactured in Europe. The French-made jet was a pioneer of the rear-mounted engine design. It began flying in 1955.

BRITISH

HB-ICJ

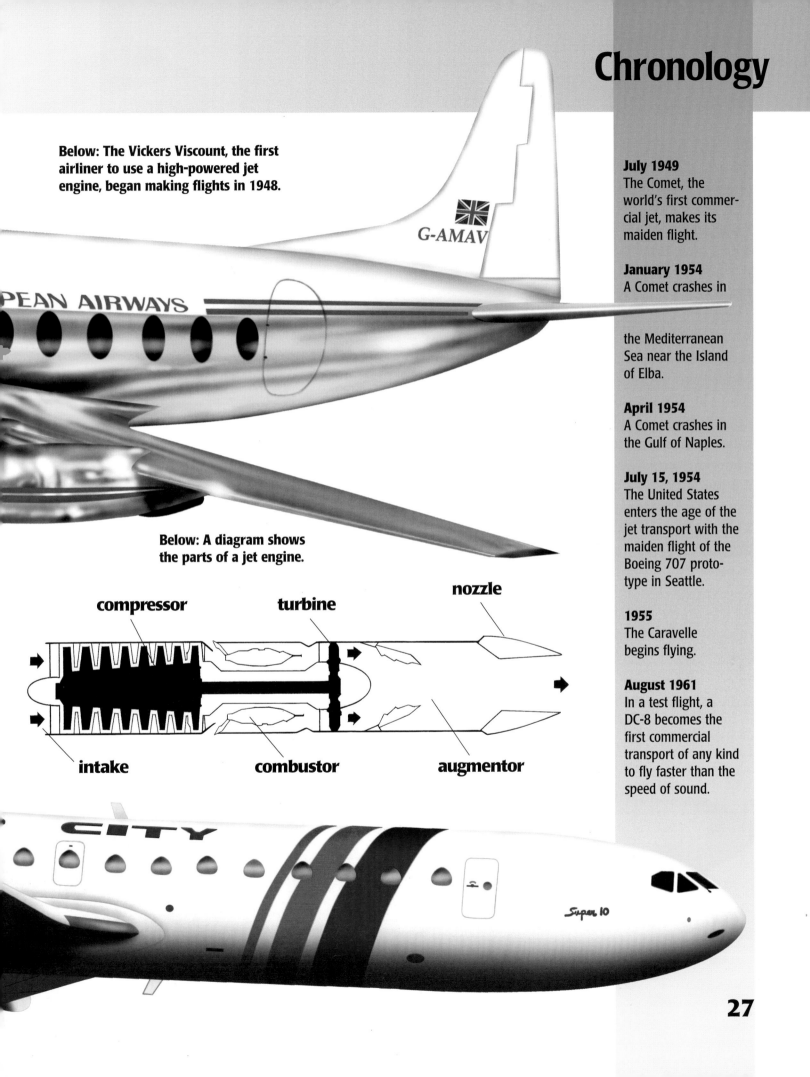

Below: The Vickers Viscount, the first airliner to use a high-powered jet engine, began making flights in 1948.

G-AMAV

PEAN AIRWAYS

Below: A diagram shows the parts of a jet engine.

compressor   turbine   nozzle

intake   combustor   augmentor

CITY

Super 10

July 1949
The Comet, the world's first commercial jet, makes its maiden flight.

January 1954
A Comet crashes in the Mediterranean Sea near the Island of Elba.

April 1954
A Comet crashes in the Gulf of Naples.

July 15, 1954
The United States enters the age of the jet transport with the maiden flight of the Boeing 707 prototype in Seattle.

1955
The Caravelle begins flying.

August 1961
In a test flight, a DC-8 becomes the first commercial transport of any kind to fly faster than the speed of sound.

Commercial airplanes did not begin using jet engines until more than two decades after their invention. The British-made de Havilland DH 106, nicknamed the Comet, was the world's first commercial jetliner. It made its first passenger flight on May 2, 1952, flying from London, England, to Johannesburg, South Africa, for the British Overseas Airway Company. The Comet flew faster than any other commercial plane at the time, reaching speeds of 500 miles (805km) per hour. It flew at higher altitudes, above the worst weather. Passengers were surprised by the lack of the noise and vibrations they had grown used to on other aircraft. However, the Comet soon experienced a number of crashes that revealed design and construction flaws. By the time the flaws were fixed, other jet designs had become more popular.

Above: A diagram shows the placement of the fuel tanks inside the wings. The large fuel tanks allow jets to cover long distances without needing to stop for more fuel.

Right: The Boeing 707 flew its first commercial voyage on December 20, 1957.

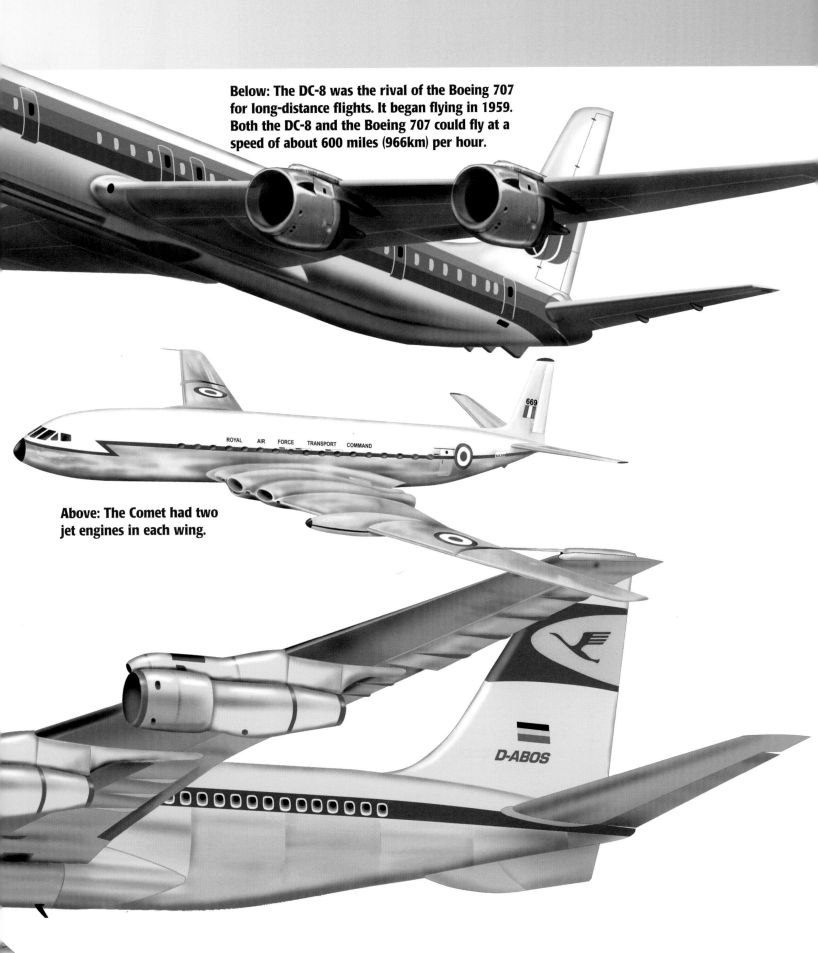

Below: The DC-8 was the rival of the Boeing 707 for long-distance flights. It began flying in 1959. Both the DC-8 and the Boeing 707 could fly at a speed of about 600 miles (966km) per hour.

Above: The Comet had two jet engines in each wing.

Giants of the Air

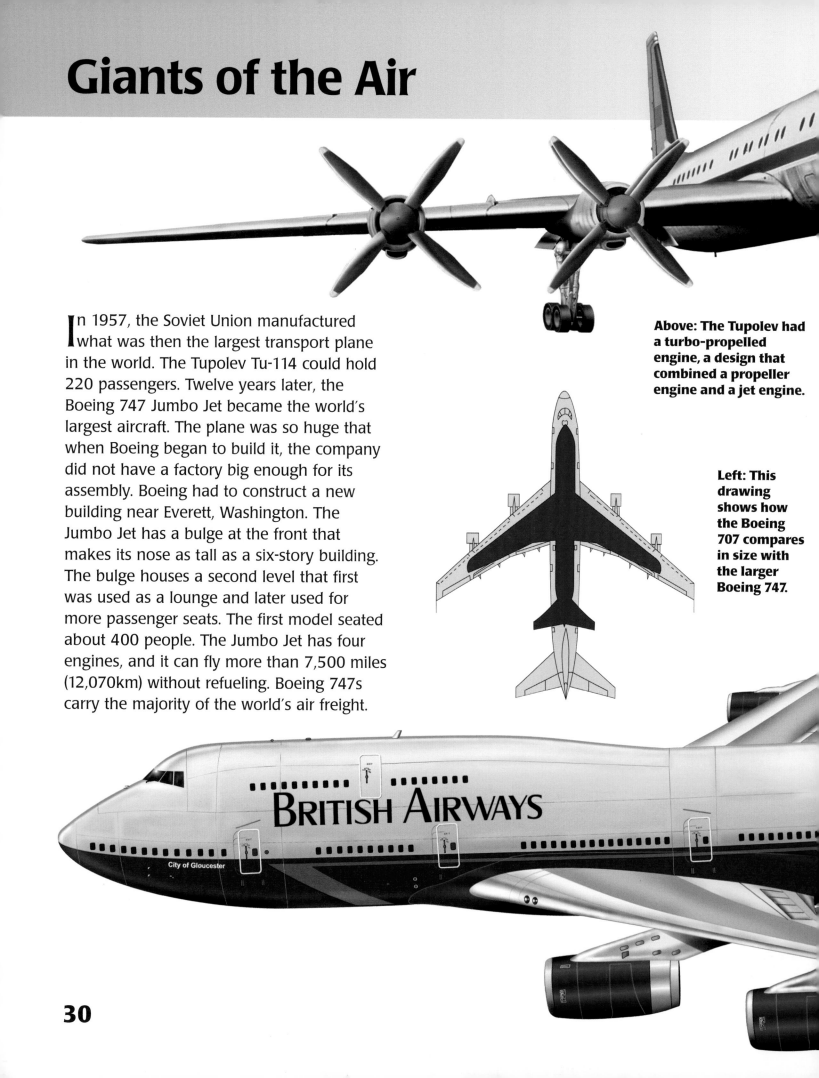

In 1957, the Soviet Union manufactured what was then the largest transport plane in the world. The Tupolev Tu-114 could hold 220 passengers. Twelve years later, the Boeing 747 Jumbo Jet became the world's largest aircraft. The plane was so huge that when Boeing began to build it, the company did not have a factory big enough for its assembly. Boeing had to construct a new building near Everett, Washington. The Jumbo Jet has a bulge at the front that makes its nose as tall as a six-story building. The bulge houses a second level that first was used as a lounge and later used for more passenger seats. The first model seated about 400 people. The Jumbo Jet has four engines, and it can fly more than 7,500 miles (12,070km) without refueling. Boeing 747s carry the majority of the world's air freight.

Above: The Tupolev had a turbo-propelled engine, a design that combined a propeller engine and a jet engine.

Left: This drawing shows how the Boeing 707 compares in size with the larger Boeing 747.

City of Gloucester

BRITISH AIRWAYS

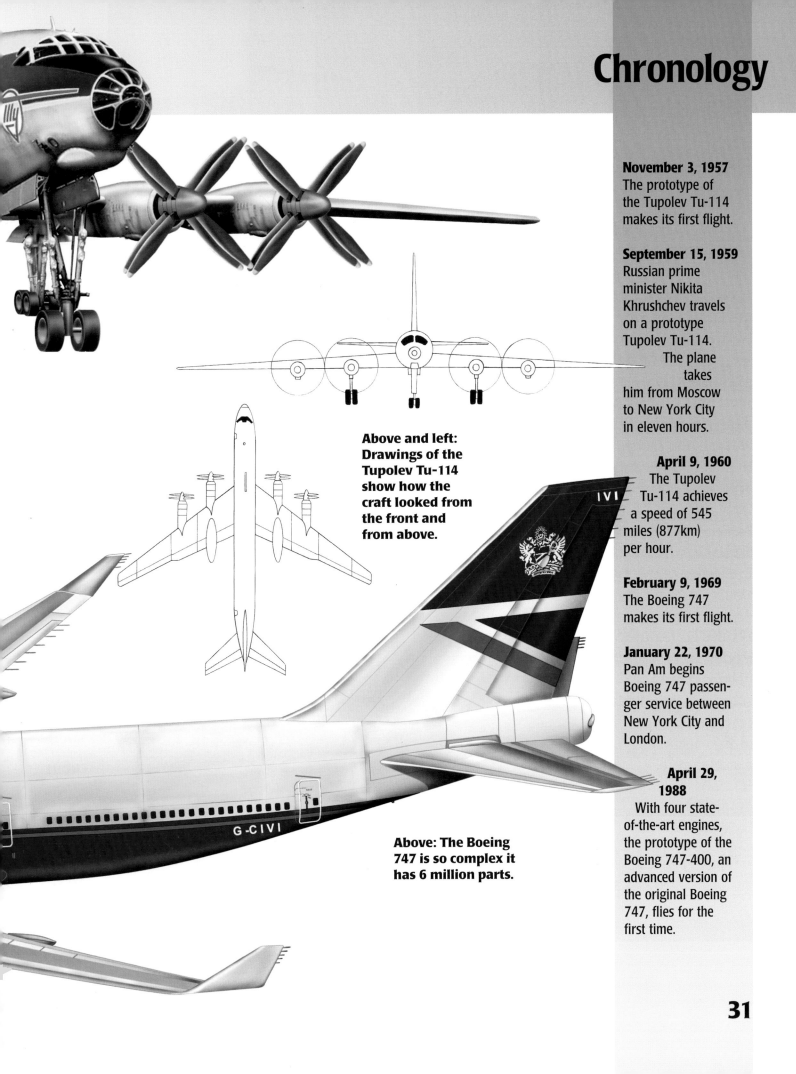

Above and left: Drawings of the Tupolev Tu-114 show how the craft looked from the front and from above.

Above: The Boeing 747 is so complex it has 6 million parts.

November 3, 1957
The prototype of the Tupolev Tu-114 makes its first flight.

September 15, 1959
Russian prime minister Nikita Khrushchev travels on a prototype Tupolev Tu-114. The plane takes him from Moscow to New York City in eleven hours.

April 9, 1960
The Tupolev Tu-114 achieves a speed of 545 miles (877km) per hour.

February 9, 1969
The Boeing 747 makes its first flight.

January 22, 1970
Pan Am begins Boeing 747 passenger service between New York City and London.

April 29, 1988
With four state-of-the-art engines, the prototype of the Boeing 747-400, an advanced version of the original Boeing 747, flies for the first time.

Helicopters

The idea of an aircraft that can fly straight up and down dates back thousands of years to toys ancient Chinese children played with. Yet the creation of the helicopter, which uses rotating blades to lift itself straight into the air, proved a very difficult task. Many aviation pioneers on many continents and over many decades worked to make the helicopter a reality. In France, brothers Louis and Jacques Breguet worked with Charles Richet to create a gyroplane in 1907. Their contraption used 32 rotating blades to rise into the air, but it was not practical. Another device was created by a German professor named Heinrich Focke. Focke designed his Focke-Wulf 61 in the 1930s, and it made its first flight on June 26, 1936. The first American helicopter was designed by Igor Sikorsky, who had immigrated to the United States from the Soviet Union. In 1940, his VS-300 became America's first successful helicopter. His design featured a large set of blades that rotated on the top of the helicopter and another, smaller set of rotating blades on the tail. His design became a standard for building modern helicopters.

Left: Leonardo da Vinci's aerial screw was one early design for a machine that used rotating blades to lift it into the air.

Above: Police officers and firefighters use helicopters because they can be piloted into places where airplanes cannot fly.

Right: The modern EC 130 helicopter can lift heavy loads. The pilot controls most of the helicopter's maneuvers with the help of a computer.

tail rotor

rotor

cabin

tail beam

skid

Chronology

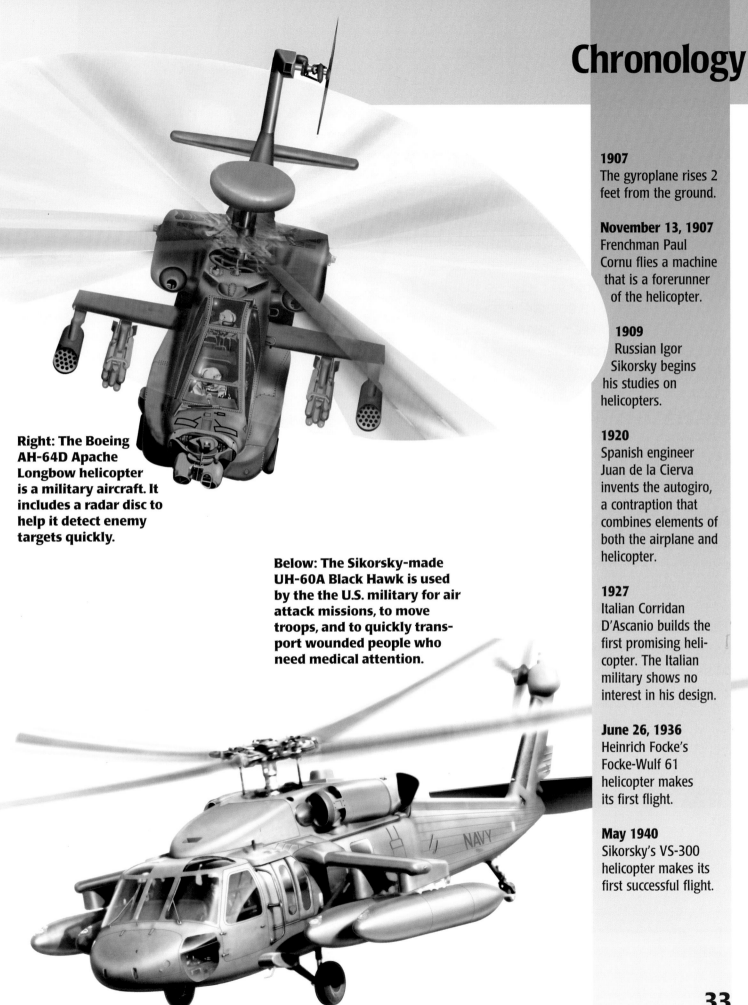

Right: The Boeing AH-64D Apache Longbow helicopter is a military aircraft. It includes a radar disc to help it detect enemy targets quickly.

Below: The Sikorsky-made UH-60A Black Hawk is used by the the U.S. military for air attack missions, to move troops, and to quickly transport wounded people who need medical attention.

1907
The gyroplane rises 2 feet from the ground.

November 13, 1907
Frenchman Paul Cornu flies a machine that is a forerunner of the helicopter.

1909
Russian Igor Sikorsky begins his studies on helicopters.

1920
Spanish engineer Juan de la Cierva invents the autogiro, a contraption that combines elements of both the airplane and helicopter.

1927
Italian Corridan D'Ascanio builds the first promising helicopter. The Italian military shows no interest in his design.

June 26, 1936
Heinrich Focke's Focke-Wulf 61 helicopter makes its first flight.

May 1940
Sikorsky's VS-300 helicopter makes its first successful flight.

Military Aircraft

Throughout history, engineers designing military aircraft have worked to make faster and better airplanes. The B-2A Spirit Strategic Stealth Bomber is a good example of an aircraft that has advanced the technology of aviation. The Stealth bomber is designed to be virtually invisible to radar, so that it is difficult for the enemy to detect the presence of the craft. The aircraft uses many devices to hide from the enemy. It uses complex electronics and a system that disguises the heat from its exhaust. It is made of materials that are difficult for detection tools to spot. Military experts describe the Stealth bomber as a flying wing. It does not have a body like other airplanes. This unusual shape also helps it to hide. The Stealth bomber carries two pilots.

The first B-2A left the assembly plant in Palmdale, California, in November 1988. It flew for the first time on July 17, 1989. The industrial and military team that created the craft won the 1991 Collier Trophy from the National Aeronautic Association. The award is given each year to honor achievements in aeronautics in the United States. Each bomber costs approximately $1.2 billion to build.

Below: The B-2A Spirit Strategic Stealth Bomber has a distinct shape that resembles a bat.

Above: The F/A-18 Hornet takes off from the ground or from aircraft carriers to patrol regions or to attack. The initials F/A in its name suggest how the plane is used. The F stands for fighter. The A stands for attack.

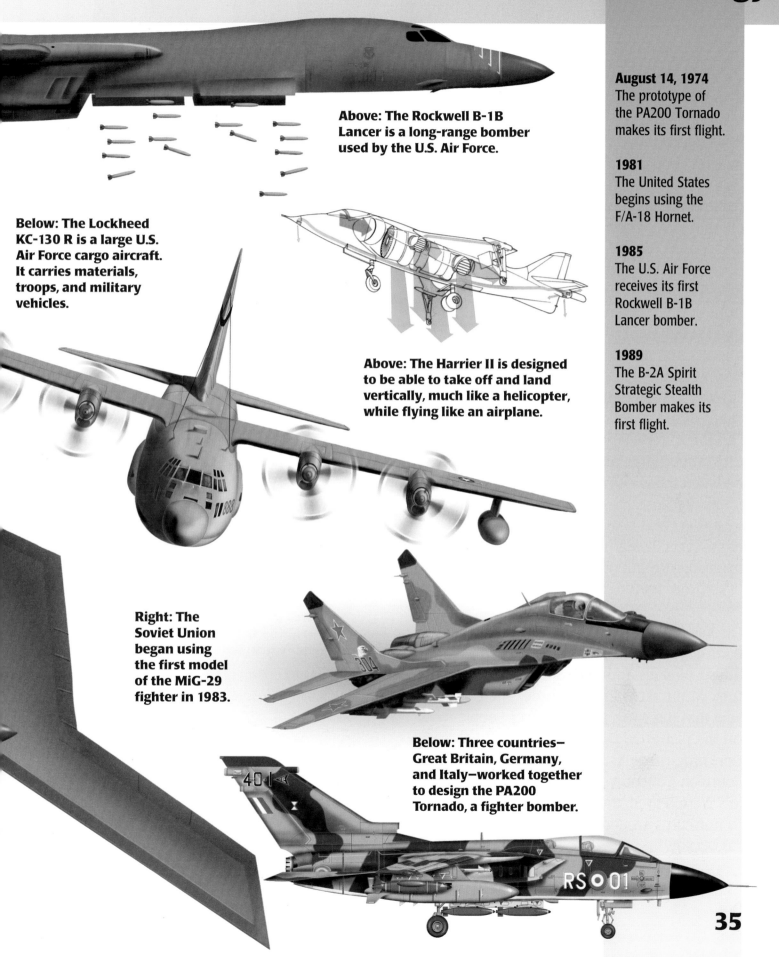

Chronology

Above: The Rockwell B-1B Lancer is a long-range bomber used by the U.S. Air Force.

Below: The Lockheed KC-130 R is a large U.S. Air Force cargo aircraft. It carries materials, troops, and military vehicles.

Above: The Harrier II is designed to be able to take off and land vertically, much like a helicopter, while flying like an airplane.

Right: The Soviet Union began using the first model of the MiG-29 fighter in 1983.

Below: Three countries—Great Britain, Germany, and Italy—worked together to design the PA200 Tornado, a fighter bomber.

August 14, 1974
The prototype of the PA200 Tornado makes its first flight.

1981
The United States begins using the F/A-18 Hornet.

1985
The U.S. Air Force receives its first Rockwell B-1B Lancer bomber.

1989
The B-2A Spirit Strategic Stealth Bomber makes its first flight.

Faster than the Speed of Sound

In 1956, researchers in Europe began working on the design of an aircraft that could fly faster than the speed of sound. The British and French governments worked together to design, develop, and manufacture the supersonic airliner. Their creation, the Concorde, flew its first commercial flight on January 21, 1976. The plane had a slender body, swept-back wings, and a nose that resembled a bird's beak. The nose bent down during take off and landing to give the pilots a better view of what was in front of them. The Concorde took off at 250 miles (402km) per hour. It flew at speeds of about 1,350 (2,173km) miles an hour. The jet flew at an altitude of more than 11 miles (18km), so high that passengers could see the curve of the earth on clear days. A flight from London to New York City aboard the Concorde took about three and a half hours. Flights between those cities usually take about eight hours. Because the Concorde used so much fuel and held only 100 passengers, flying on it was very expensive. In 2000, a round-trip ticket from Paris to New York City cost $8,148.

On July 25, 2000, a Concorde crashed near Paris, killing 113 people. Within three years, British Airways and Air France announced that they would retire the Concorde. The company said that the crash had led fewer people to fly on the plane. On October 24, 2003, the Concorde made its last commercial flights. Fourteen Concordes were flown. After the jets were retired, they were sent to museums around the world for display.

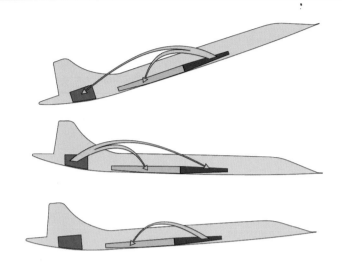

Above: The Concorde's center of gravity had to be changed at different stages of flights for the plane to fly safely. To do this, fuel was transferred to different tanks throughout the plane.

Above: The Concorde's takeoff speed was 250 miles per hour. The plane's cruising speed was 1,350 miles per hour, more than twice the speed of sound.

Chronology

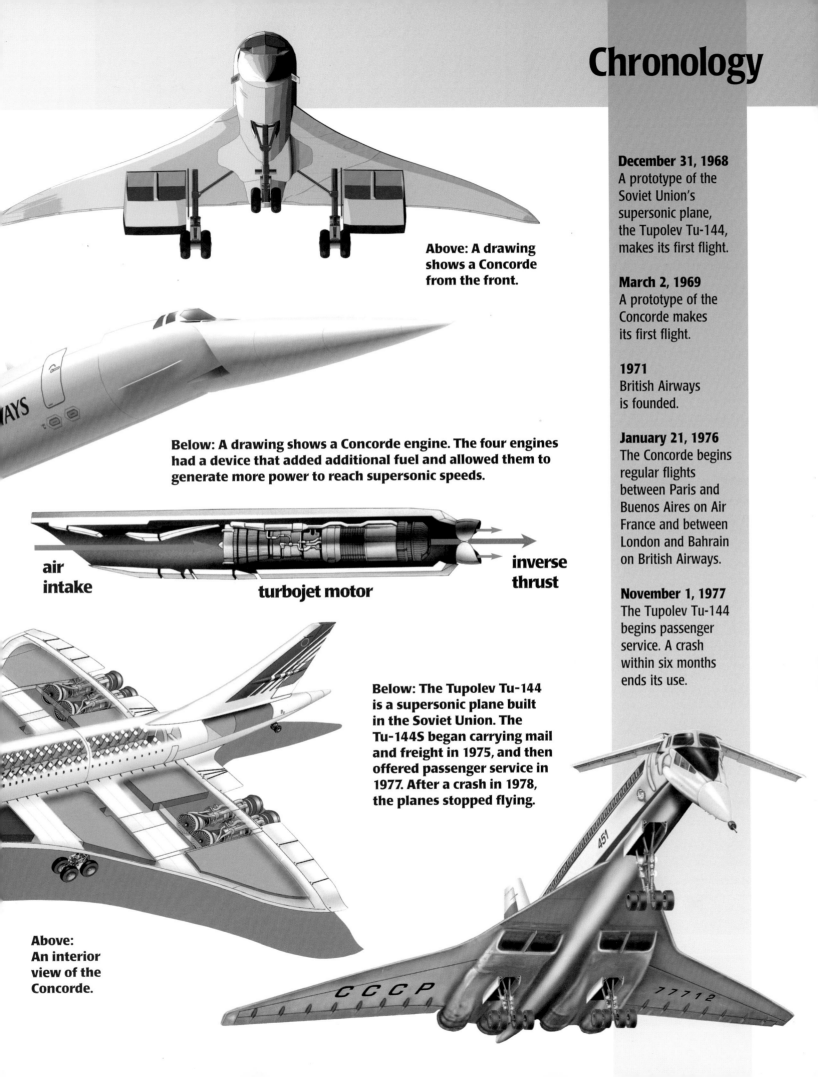

Above: A drawing shows a Concorde from the front.

Below: A drawing shows a Concorde engine. The four engines had a device that added additional fuel and allowed them to generate more power to reach supersonic speeds.

air intake

turbojet motor

inverse thrust

Below: The Tupolev Tu-144 is a supersonic plane built in the Soviet Union. The Tu-144S began carrying mail and freight in 1975, and then offered passenger service in 1977. After a crash in 1978, the planes stopped flying.

Above: An interior view of the Concorde.

December 31, 1968
A prototype of the Soviet Union's supersonic plane, the Tupolev Tu-144, makes its first flight.

March 2, 1969
A prototype of the Concorde makes its first flight.

1971
British Airways is founded.

January 21, 1976
The Concorde begins regular flights between Paris and Buenos Aires on Air France and between London and Bahrain on British Airways.

November 1, 1977
The Tupolev Tu-144 begins passenger service. A crash within six months ends its use.

The Next Giant

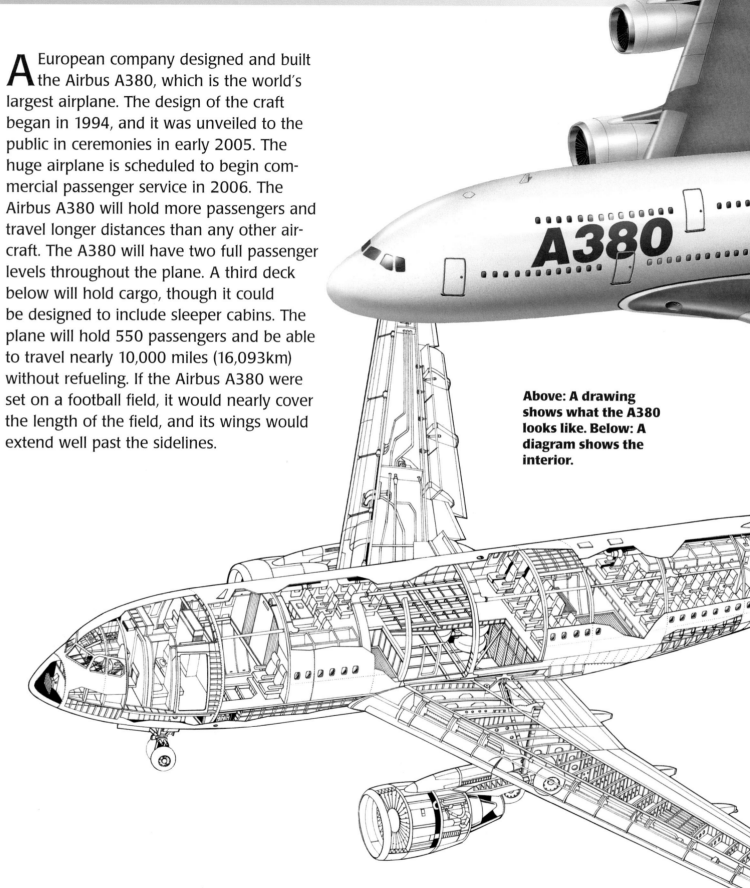

A European company designed and built the Airbus A380, which is the world's largest airplane. The design of the craft began in 1994, and it was unveiled to the public in ceremonies in early 2005. The huge airplane is scheduled to begin commercial passenger service in 2006. The Airbus A380 will hold more passengers and travel longer distances than any other aircraft. The A380 will have two full passenger levels throughout the plane. A third deck below will hold cargo, though it could be designed to include sleeper cabins. The plane will hold 550 passengers and be able to travel nearly 10,000 miles (16,093km) without refueling. If the Airbus A380 were set on a football field, it would nearly cover the length of the field, and its wings would extend well past the sidelines.

Above: A drawing shows what the A380 looks like. Below: A diagram shows the interior.

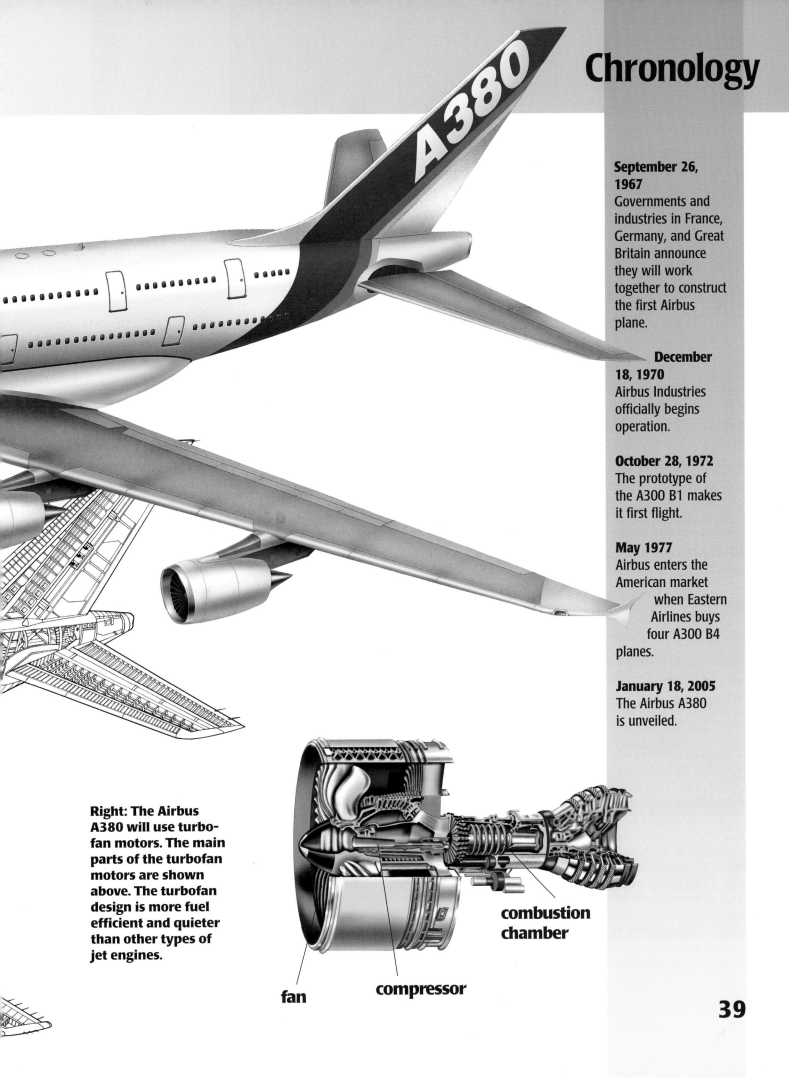

September 26, 1967
Governments and industries in France, Germany, and Great Britain announce they will work together to construct the first Airbus plane.

December 18, 1970
Airbus Industries officially begins operation.

October 28, 1972
The prototype of the A300 B1 makes it first flight.

May 1977
Airbus enters the American market when Eastern Airlines buys four A300 B4 planes.

January 18, 2005
The Airbus A380 is unveiled.

Right: The Airbus A380 will use turbo-fan motors. The main parts of the turbofan motors are shown above. The turbofan design is more fuel efficient and quieter than other types of jet engines.

combustion chamber

fan

compressor

Into Space

On April 12, 1961, the Soviet cosmonaut Yuri Alekseyevich Gagarin became the first person to travel in space. He orbited the Earth in the capsule *Vostok I* for 108 minutes. Eight years later, on July 20, 1969, U.S. astronaut Neil Armstrong became the first person to walk on the Moon. "That's one small step for [a] man, one giant leap for mankind," Armstrong said as he stepped onto the lunar surface. He described the soil on the Moon's surface as resembling powder.

Armstrong was the commander of a spacecraft called *Apollo 11*. Three astronauts went in the spacecraft: Armstrong, Edwin Buzz Aldrin, and Michael Collins. Armstrong and Aldrin went to the Moon in a special module, while Collins circled the moon in the command craft. Armstrong and Aldrin spent about two and a half hours outside their module, collecting samples of the Moon's rocks and soil and taking photographs. Their mission fulfilled President John F. Kennedy's goal of landing a person on the Moon before the end of the 1960s. The astronauts left behind an American flag and a plaque that reads, "Here Men From Planet Earth First Set Foot Upon the Moon July 1969 A.D. We Came in Peace For All Mankind." When the astronauts returned to Earth on July 24, they were welcomed as heroes.

Right: Drawings show stages of progress of the *Apollo 11* as it prepares to send a module to the Moon. The Saturn V rocket that launched *Apollo 11* had separate fuel stages—a combination of engines and fuel—that were detached after the fuel inside them had been used. (1) The second stage of the rocket detaches. (2) The command module, the *Columbia*, detaches and turns. (3) The *Columbia* reattaches to the lunar excursion module (LEM), the *Eagle*. (4) The third stage of the rocket detaches. (5) The *Eagle* leaves the *Columbia* command module to prepare to land on the Moon.

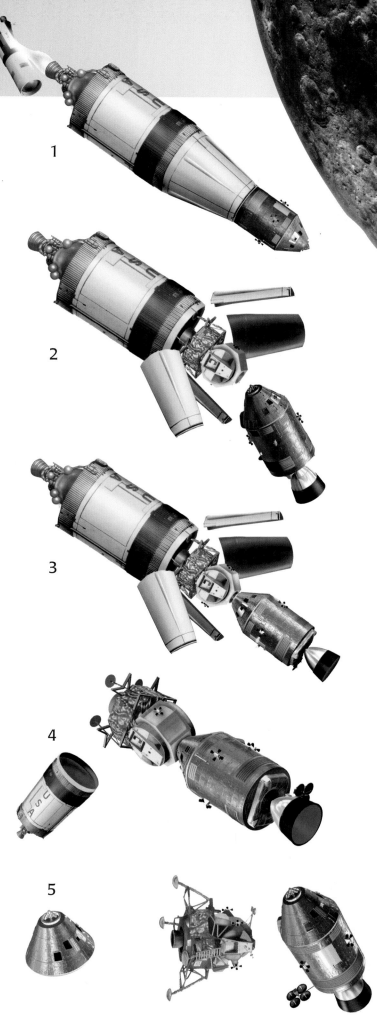

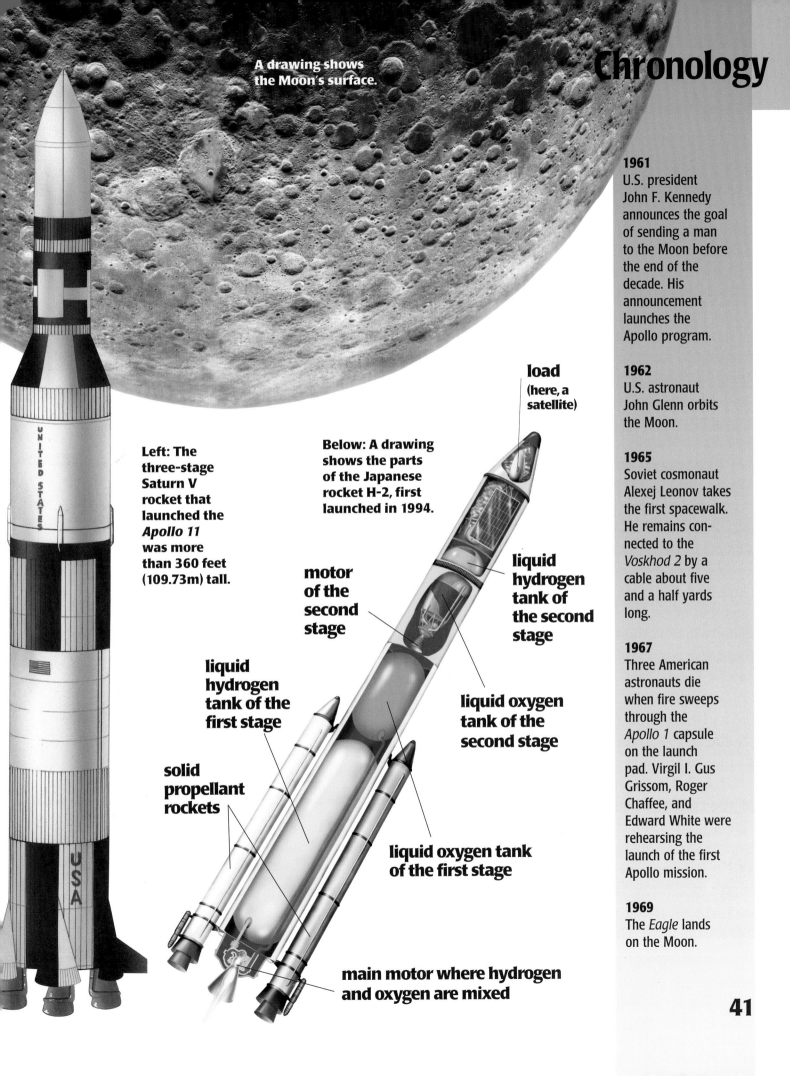

A drawing shows the Moon's surface.

load
(here, a satellite)

Left: The three-stage Saturn V rocket that launched the *Apollo 11* was more than 360 feet (109.73m) tall.

Below: A drawing shows the parts of the Japanese rocket H-2, first launched in 1994.

UNITED STATES

USA

motor of the second stage

liquid hydrogen tank of the second stage

liquid hydrogen tank of the first stage

liquid oxygen tank of the second stage

solid propellant rockets

liquid oxygen tank of the first stage

main motor where hydrogen and oxygen are mixed

1961
U.S. president John F. Kennedy announces the goal of sending a man to the Moon before the end of the decade. His announcement launches the Apollo program.

1962
U.S. astronaut John Glenn orbits the Moon.

1965
Soviet cosmonaut Alexej Leonov takes the first spacewalk. He remains connected to the *Voskhod 2* by a cable about five and a half yards long.

1967
Three American astronauts die when fire sweeps through the *Apollo 1* capsule on the launch pad. Virgil I. Gus Grissom, Roger Chaffee, and Edward White were rehearsing the launch of the first Apollo mission.

1969
The *Eagle* lands on the Moon.

Space Shuttles

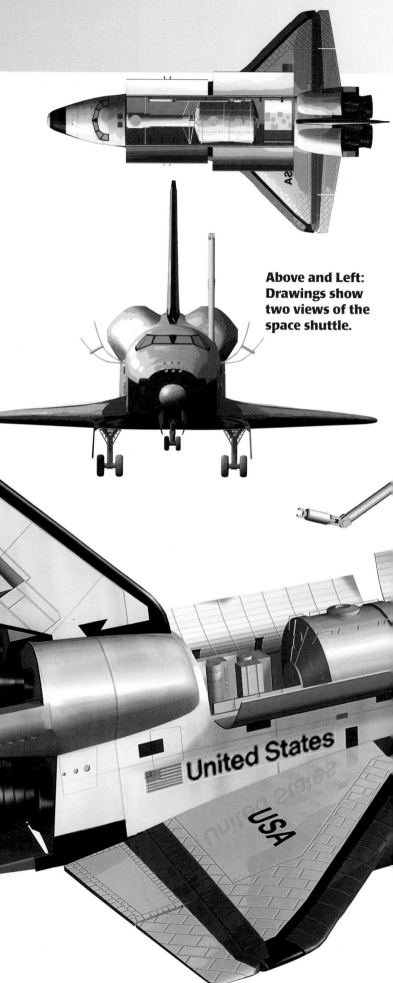

On April 12, 1981, the U.S. space agency NASA launched a new type of spacecraft called the space shuttle. The space shuttle was the first spacecraft designed to be partly reusable. All earlier spacecraft could be used only one time. Until the space shuttle was created, astronauts returned to Earth in capsules that fell into the ocean. The space shuttle was designed to return to Earth and to land like an airplane. The original idea behind the shuttle was to create a manned spacecraft that could fly frequently, cost less than other space vehicles, and be more reliable.

Above and Left: Drawings show two views of the space shuttle.

The space shuttle has four main parts. The reusable orbiter is the part that looks like a plane. There is a huge outside fuel tank that is detached after its fuel is used. There are also two reusable booster rockets that are filled with solid fuel. They are also detached and then recovered so they can be used again.

Research on what became the space shuttle began in the late 1960s. Five shuttles were built. Two of them were destroyed in accidents that killed all the crew members aboard. On January 28, 1986, the *Challenger* exploded 73 seconds after it lifted off, killing the seven people aboard. On February 1, 2003, the *Columbia* exploded as it was returning to Earth. Seven astronauts were killed in that disaster.

Chronology

Below and Right:
A drawing shows the space shuttle. Its cargo bay can hold many materials, including satellites and telescopes.

April 12, 1981
The space shuttle takes its first flight.

January 28, 1986
The *Challenger* explodes, killing seven people aboard. The space shuttle program is temporarily halted.

November 15, 1988
The Soviet Union launches its first unmanned shuttle, named *Buran*, meaning snowstorm or blizzard. Though its launch is successful, the program stops with the collapse of the Soviet Union and a lack of funding.

October 30, 1998
John Glenn, the first astronaut to orbit the moon, returns to space at the age of 77 on board the space shuttle *Discovery*.

February 1, 2003
The *Columbia* explodes as it returns to Earth.

Right: When the shuttle takes off, it goes straight up. It weighs 2,000 tons. After the fuel tank and two rocket boosters detach, it looks like an airplane. It then weighs 69 tons.

43

Airplanes of the Future

Left: NASA is testing a prototype of the Helios, an unmanned solar-powered aircraft. The agency hopes these aircraft will be a low-cost alternative to current space-based satellites.

No one knows exactly what the airplanes of the future will be like. Some engineers are working on ways to make the next generation of airplanes nearly silent. Some engineers are trying to design planes that use less fuel. Other engineers are trying to design planes that are bigger. Still other engineers are trying to design planes that can fly faster.

At Boeing, one of the world's leading aircraft manufacturers, designers are working on a 250-seat jet that can travel almost as fast as the speed of sound. In March 2001, the company unveiled plans to build the Sonic Cruiser.. The wings and fins of the plane are arranged in a unique way that gives the plane an unusual look. The company says its plane will be able to fly at about 660 miles (1,062km) per hour and will cut travel times by about 20 percent, or one hour for every 3,000 miles (4,828km) traveled. And because it is designed to travel at higher altitudes than existing commercial jets, the Sonic Cruiser will be able to fly at altitudes with less air traffic congestion.

Above: A drawing shows the unusual wings and tail of the proposed Boeing Sonic Cruiser.

Below: NASA's High Speed Research Program is trying to design a commercial jet that can make supersonic travel affordable.

44

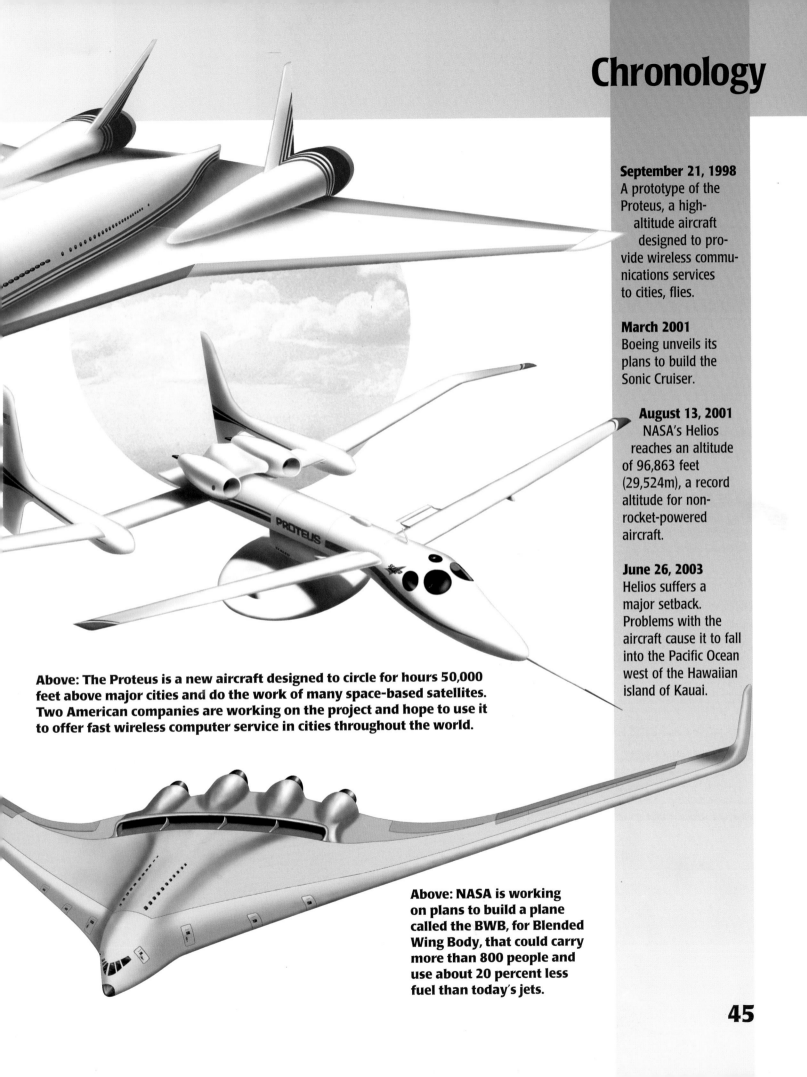

September 21, 1998
A prototype of the Proteus, a high-altitude aircraft designed to provide wireless communications services to cities, flies.

March 2001
Boeing unveils its plans to build the Sonic Cruiser.

August 13, 2001
NASA's Helios reaches an altitude of 96,863 feet (29,524m), a record altitude for non-rocket-powered aircraft.

June 26, 2003
Helios suffers a major setback. Problems with the aircraft cause it to fall into the Pacific Ocean west of the Hawaiian island of Kauai.

Above: The Proteus is a new aircraft designed to circle for hours 50,000 feet above major cities and do the work of many space-based satellites. Two American companies are working on the project and hope to use it to offer fast wireless computer service in cities throughout the world.

Above: NASA is working on plans to build a plane called the BWB, for Blended Wing Body, that could carry more than 800 people and use about 20 percent less fuel than today's jets.

Glossary

aeronautics: The technology and science of operating aircraft.

aircraft carrier: A warship used to carry aircraft. Aircraft can take off and land from its large deck.

airship: A self-powered, lighter-than-air craft that can be steered.

altitude: Height above sea level.

atmosphere: The mixture of gases that surround the Earth, another planet, or other celestial body, such as a star.

aviation: The design, development, and production of aircraft.

blimp: An informal name for a kind of airship that is different from a zeppelin. The blimp does not have a rigid structure. It usually uses helium, a lighter-than-air gas, to keep it in flight.

bomber: An aircraft that carries and drops bombs.

cockpit: The part of the plane where the pilot sits.

fighter: A small, fast aircraft used to attack and destroy enemy aircraft.

glider: A light plane without engines.

hydrogen: A gas that is lighter than air.

jet engine: A powerful type of engine that gives aircraft the power to fly at high speeds.

landing gear: The wheels and wheel supports of an aircraft.

orbit: To revolve around an object. The Earth, for example, orbits the Sun.

pressurize: To maintain normal air pressure in an aircraft flying at high altitudes.

prototype: A full-scale, working model of a new device or a new model of an existing device.

radar: A device that uses radio waves to detect distant objects.

route: A line of travel between two points.

satellite: A man-made object launched to orbit Earth.

speed of sound: The speed at which a sound wave travels. The speed of sound varies with conditions in the atmosphere, such as altitude and temperature.

stealth: Having the ability to avoid detection by radar.

supersonic: Able to travel faster than the speed of sound.

turbine: A rotary engine that uses a continuous stream of fluid, such as gas, to drive the engine.

wind tunnel: A tunnel through which air is blown to test the flow of air around objects placed in the tunnel.

zeppelin: An airship that used hydrogen, a gas that is lighter than air, to help it fly.

For More Information

Glen and Karen Bledsoe, *The World's Fastest Helicopters.* Mankato, MN: Capstone, 2002.

Carmen Bredeson, *Living on a Space Shuttle.* New York: Children's Press, 2003.

Ann Byers, *The Crash of the Concorde.* New York: Rosen Central, 2003.

Mark Dartford, *Bombers.* Minneapolis, MN: Lerner, 2003.

Mindi Rose Englart, *Helicopters: From Start to Finish.* San Diego, CA: Blackbirch Press, 2003.

Michael and Gladys Green, *Stealth Attack Fighters: The F-117A Nighthawks.* Mankato, MN: Capstone, 2003.

Ole Steen Hansen, *Military Aircraft of WWII.* New York: Crabtree, 2003.

Henry M. Holden, *The Supersonic X-15 and High-Tech NASA Aircraft.* Berkeley Heights, NJ: Enslow, 2002.

———, *The Tragedy of the Space Shuttle Challenger.* Berkeley Heights, NJ: MyReportLinks.com Books, 2004.

Victoria Sherrow, *The Hindenburg Disaster: Doomed Airship.* Berkeley Heights, NJ: Enslow, 2002.

Bill Sweetman, *High-Altitude Spy Planes: The U-2s.* Mankato, MN: Capstone, 2001.

Sheila Wyborny, *The Wright Brothers.* San Diego, CA: KidHaven Press, 2003.

Index